7/14/2006
To Anselm,
with love.
xo M

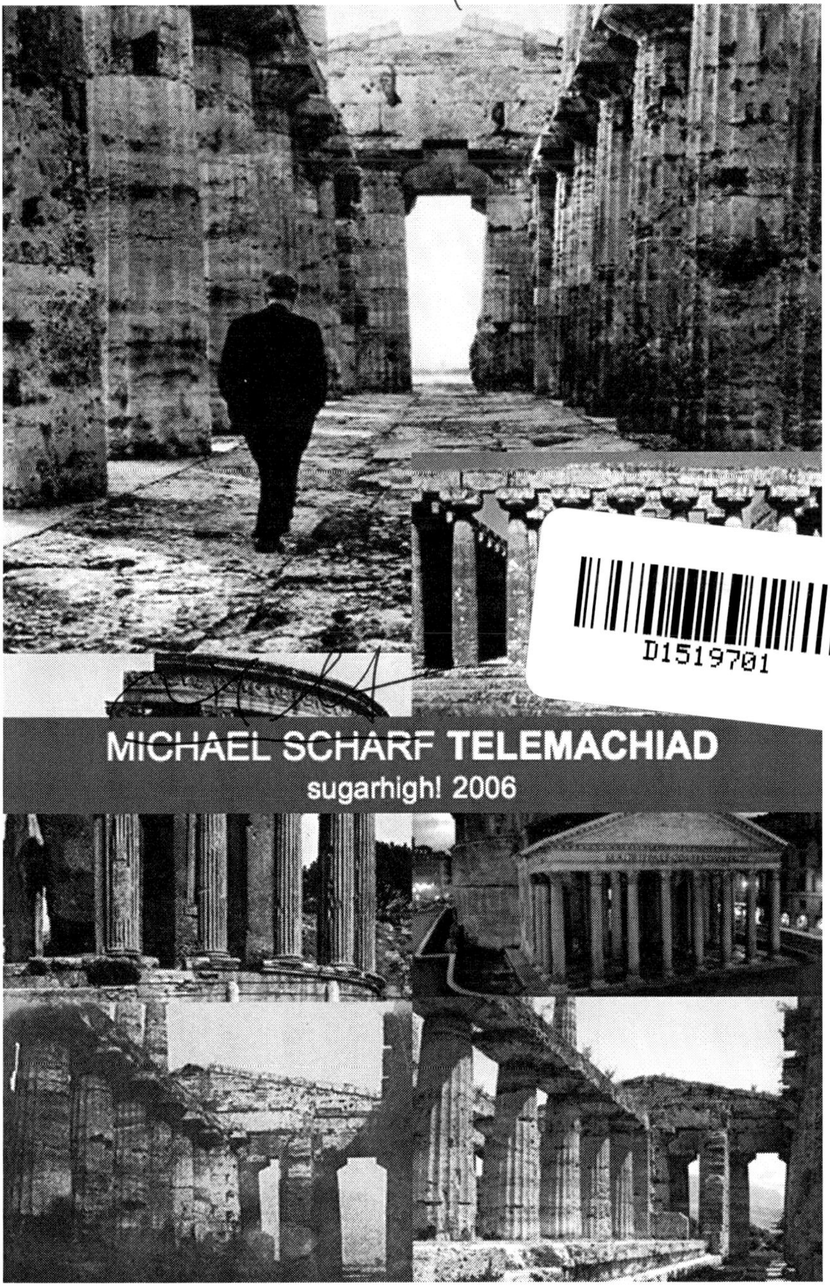

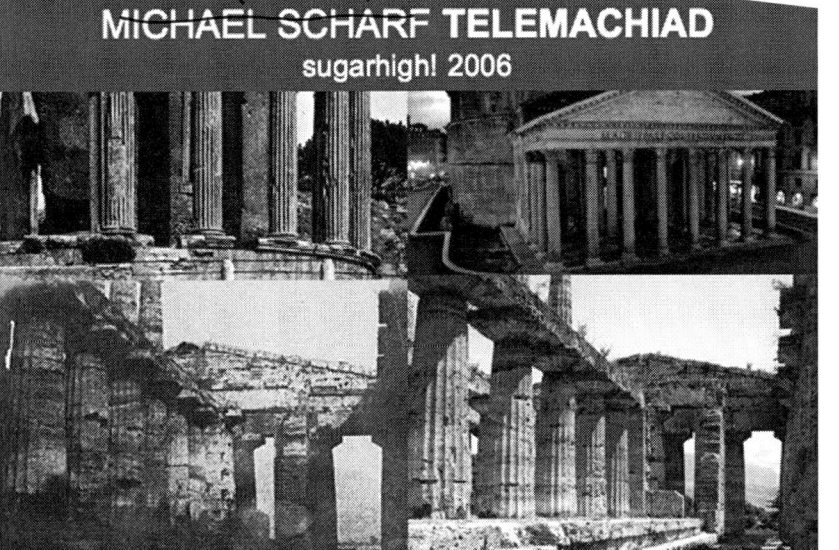

MICHAEL SCHARF TELEMACHIAD
sugarhigh! 2006

© 1999 Michael Scharf
© 2006 sugarhigh!

Cover Image: *Sacramento Tree* © 2005 by Brandon Downing

Frontispieces by Jennifer Wolfe

Telemachiad published ("in New York during Elul") in 1999
for the subpoetics self-publish or perish project

"FTP" published by *The East Village*

Nine Sonnets beautifully published by xPressed.org in 2003

The Spicer lament published by who other than *Mirage #4/Period(ical)*

Three-book edition first published by sugarhigh! in 2004

"The Lecture," "Recording Over," and "Snow" published
by *The Germ*

"Lilies in Beds Take Control of the Dead" is for Dan Farrell.

"Recording Over" is for Brian Kim Stefans.

ISBN 0-9678031-9-5

TO BE PLAYED AT MAXIMUM VOLUME

Telemachiad

ERRING ALONE

I was relating it to myself
and the morning came; I was wild
restored
some 450 type-written pages,
major symbol activities.
Thoughts of death and related contents
keep careful track of ideation,
that almost diabolical moral "virtue."
Removed from contact
for the first thirty-six hours
"contamination" for anyone possessing
psychoanalytic knowledge.

Third of nine born—
this one stubborn, that one cold
living
abroad.
Peculiarities become
conspicuous
during the first six to eight weeks—
fixed, rather tense, positions.
A choppy
at times explosive
billowing—
a mutinous scramble in the wood;
a secret career as a drinker
airing a lone—vache.
The other two,
rather revengeful,
to a college in New York City—
psychiatric lecture on December 5.

Venice in June can be hell
featured prominently for a time in my dreams
deposited in a small cupboard-like space
elsewhere.

A torturous and difficult maneuver;
a flourishing

gambling establishment, similarly
sized department store.
I was slightly excited,
under the domination and guidance of a milk-
white star, vaguely
identified with the patient.

I worked very hard and faithfully;
I worked apparently for hours at the useless
task, another fantasy
clearly recalled.

Miss S., Mrs. Jack Johnson, is clearly
the mother ideal, festooned with chips and other
paraphernalia. *Inter alia.*

Flying in close embrace with a coward
very much opposed to treatment
Mr. K, the voluptuous Jewess, with a pocket
full of dockets, cessna-ing
from one luxuriant valley to another,
points to the hospital.

In a subsequent discussion,
I tried to treat everyone square;
I was supposed to be in hell I guess;
They had a language there;
I'd hear things;
I couldn't smoke a cigarette or drink water.

This fly I termed a 'Benjamin Franklin'
fly,
superhuman
prowess, precise antics
on the top of the table.

The parents stubborn, living
abroad. What
life with them must have
been like.

A burdensome
package
sheathed in your kindness,
your willingness to help in even
the most difficult circumstances,
a
sort
of
Tarantinan 'Wolf' of my fantasies.

He gave me what is known as the "queen's salute."
Flying rapidly over the surface of the earth
locked in close sexual embrace,
luxuriant
evidence.

If Brian's poetry is what's
behind all of this, what will
you think of my sources?
It's the obvious question, as politically
motivated as "Of Being Numerous,"
with its plumes of smoke,
or
the anthologizing of the Todesfugue.

Relentlessly assertive of truth,
the try;
the heartbreakingly freighted arrival;
the uncompromising, line-broken noun
carrying the spavined consciousness.

Business relations
night terrors, temper tantrums, enuresis, etc.

They had become so active
and were so given
to standing while in a carriage, or car
they were burned by turning over
a container of hot potatoes.

Very nervous and restless,
they suffered a great deal, resembling
each other in physique and physiognomy
strikingly.

My feelings have got swung around.
I was relating it to myself
and the morning came,
talked through clothes and automobiles;
all our actions and talks
were tensions between us
meaning this,
a bolt out. No, you can't...
stop that, but... I suppose
you can choose the right time. Number '4'
to my mind, '4' is sort of a doctor's
number. I touched the 4-ball.

For my new friend, Jack Spicer, Who couldn't Spot a Jew

I

Just what you would have wanted
—a collected. But "Foxy-boy
Sortie" and "Champ by
and of the Mouth" have been excised.

Your heart turns over
sends uncharacteristically bourgeois
demons down

My stuffed animals and your shit bag.

II

The tractatus;

The practicum; the pronouns;

The bedspread dropping to the floor;

The endless texts of the 60s;

At that age I said
"I'm a real tomboy!"

The comforting texts of the 60s,

the mail dropped onto the floor.

I yawned back and smelled the pheromones
on the top
of my lip.

Beautiful, sensitive
responsive
but
may have a message
beyond
a
small
clop.

III

It echoed in the big house,
the woodpecker knocking his brains out on the dead tree.

Neither child nor nursery be;

Decommission the Irish Sea;

We are certainly free—

sold and bartered on the strand
yet clearly unfettered—

A door closed. It echoed up the stairs and raised
the animal's hairs.

There is a slight knocking;
it is the endless texts of the 60s.

IV

I read the manifestoes out loud to my children.

I went out of the house. There were leaves on the ground
and a light rain falling.

In Nottingham the tea goes "Tsk." In Manchester they discuss Man
United.
I wanted a cozy.

The wood floors echoed after the next operation, which removed me
from the grass and brought me into the house.

His or her behind
brave, jocund, unfeeling.

"Batterny batterny batterny, the stones of blarney go—"

V

Be bop de beep
the kitty
and the creep
outrun allusions

He has always been an obvious thinker
rigidly attracted to received opinion.

He was an antenna of his era, a transceiver
delicately tuned to the tenor of his times.

Who are the sons of Bruce, and why do we love them?

VI

Touched by an anglophone.
And... I... touches... what's-his-name
put the three ball in the pocket.
Homophonic literature
seizing upon furniture
upon the music of my work.
If I can't touch you here in this place
of near precocity, altruism
and blindness, and can't furtively catch
the sleeve of some passing monstrosity
to what will you chalk up my panic?
The small, hard hairs of chin? The dog's antic
pull, waxing the sidewalk with leg dips
and a full-on kiss to the garbage lips?

I reach for your cake, end up with your hands.
I can't help but feel good, meet all demands.

VII

Steve,
the same Steve who appears throughout
said "we're having an exchange
right now" at dinner. I'm giddy right now
at this powerful allusion, dressed carefully
for that dinner.

Qently to my chambur in Chambord
I removed the skis. In alien corn
under alien skies the French looked at me.
The floor flooded a quarter-inch
before the shock
of lip lock.

VIII

My beliefs run from
the tinkling streams to the facile depths
in the light of several decorums.
Sitting in men's chairs
performing verbal ablutions
I move in the space of actual hairs,
avoid the well-heeled stool-sitters
and head down for a pee.

Comport, belie, tryst.
Lenses, brush, bust
and dial. Cloy, file and
tines. Mist, paper, rack
float.

So that's what your back looks like,
and below, your pants fit right.
Shirtless
tight
in the way you move your arms, the little
death, the thin straps of your tank,
a satisfied shrug I can't mimic.

IX

I press the bar that makes
the clock tell the time.
It's 6:08.

It's a mass-market sunrise.
Links from the dictionary
to the fruitbowl. A slight hectoring
buzz. A mound of folded yawl.

Seer sucker.
Plink of experience.
Connote and commode
extension from one life into the next
from comportment to the stocking
department, from the elevator
to the shoes.

Boring you with truthful demonstrations
of melon and softer flesh.

X

Brits: big louts
clouting
each other.

If I were
        receiving the swan;
    if I were
the receiving swan—

"I've been fucking
seeing patients all day
& you
want me to what?"

Haw
haw
—ahem.

We feel;
death creams.

XI

Language as a model! To think everything through in terms
        of linguistics!
An unconscious structured like a language! Language evolved
        for proximity.
Will-to-power is bringing others to you! Language is a real thing
        that requires
you to put yourself in an imaginary relationship to it. The form
        of the poem is
the poet's body. Blank verse holds Wrdswrth together, with little
        o-rings.
Sentences are built in expectation of an argument, and assign
        thematic roles.
Good Will Hunting was a terrific movie about a genius; he took
        things in stride.
Can X afford Y though, as an idea? Dissonance between proximal
        availability
('Little Neck Clams') and distal unavailability of the poet
        (Little Neck Clams).
The author widens the scope or shucks the bake for a price.
        You want to ask Matt:
Why English is iambically friendly? Because nouns are head final:
        NP —> Det N.

XII

Shissyfuss puthes
da wock.
—Shut your fucking mouth.

Gene says "wiff"
and I jump.
Imperthn—

moth
my mowff

Mima and Matt
their mother
impossibly beautiful

"Go Climb a Rock"
I cld barely
grip my d—
at that age.

XIII

Park poetry, social.

XIV

Where's the eros? The real rotting birdy?
Van Gogh's "Pair of Boobs"

Until the medium stabilizes
That is, microtizes,
Won't reproduce.
Xerxes PARC

a sow's ear.
a roc's egg.
a hero's welcome.
a king's ransom.

XV

My mother worked at the Magic Circle Bookshop. Before that
she had had another boyfriend, named Art, who had a VW bug
with a sunroof. He poked his hand out and waved to me as we
drove in separate cars to Old Westbury Gardens. The gardens
were real; Art was nice.

TELEMACHIAD

If your spavined, broken-winded horse can't
clop into town under its own steam
and gets overtaken by another man's wagon,
you have to wonder who'll be picking through the porn,
bowling trophies, frozen chicken boxes
and half-squeezed bottles of Afrin.

So fucked up on whatever drugs kept you vertical,
so terrifying in your proppings of me, with giant hairy arms,
follicles organized in semitic rivulets, you stood;
"hundreds and hundreds" of women
leaned behind you as you threw each ball—
custom drilled, engraved, sixteen pounds—
putting out. Pretty much all you could eat
was cantaloupe, and if you ate steak—

So now I'm gently shoveling the dirt myself
chasing away the morons with the backhoe,
and if you're watching
if you want to give me a little nod,
some sticky phrase translated into COBOL
and rapped out onto punch cards,

if you are unable to drink alcohol or work for Ira
by the light of your unarticulated class
aversions, your inability to reach across
the table and touch my grandfather's velvet lapel
tenderly, like a rabbit's ear, or talk substantively
about analysis or algorithm, though you made the latter
for a living and performed the former sexually—
by that light—

This stuff is endless.
Ex voto
ab ovo,
"hyper"
not "energetic."

I'm wrenching things into shape,
but to you I hope
it's pretty clear

When my father
comes into contact with dogwood blossoms
or a hive
of cellophane-wrapped Jack Spicer,
a mummy

I pipe orphically;
I burst into song;
I cry at the sight of abject men

The explosive trees,
quietly popping into bloom,
pooping on the toilet—
and those talking birds
must have been little girls.

Schreber, Schubert, Sch—Don't touch it!
Endured countless "honest moments"
I'm coming into my own!

You're not listening
and the trees, for all their spread, couldn't
really give a crap. But little by little,
the talking birds reassert themselves,
and Schreber's relationship with his dead

father resolves
into brotherly affection, before his
brother,

too, dies and Schreber
offers himself
to the rays of God.
Lighting farts in burnt offering,
lavishly firing

toward a loved one,

failing to repress even the faintest of stirrings,
kicking the crazy door of the jakes,

disbelief about scatology
turns to eschatology, ontology;
the bubble turns its mirrors onto the people
from the mount;
essences turn to empires

and all that was
 reduced, unsung,
    bloated,

unrelieve
-d
comes pouring out. But
for
what? Let

comfort
unmake
you.

Epithal-Epistle

I would be brilliant;
I had nothing on mind;
passed the mirror a fourth time,
saw the symbols inscribed, follicle
by follicle. On pointe, then plié.
Shave. You
loaded each phrase with a rhetorical texture

so rich, any recasting of mine
would seem purposeful, clumsy.
The more I
stare at the photo the more
it gives up. Brush.

Pack. Little bits of toast;
small francophile wants;
aristocratic filth; tines;
Daddy's letters;
Nolan's towels.

After last week's running around
as long as we're together and actively close
we're not going to be ecstatic all the time
it was sort of riotous
yet of course not insurmountable
joy; aqua-velvum; aviator;
Nolan's towels.

This summer we lived in a kind of spiral
and the world was ours.
When we separated in the physical sense
our world of together impressions and reactions
was put in abeyance.

Passed the mirror a fourth time
saw the symbols inscribed, follicle by
follicle. Baroque detail.
When we were together our plans for the future
were almost materialized

since we jumped from summer to summer
it shows up in sort of a grasping way.
Because of the physical distance between us,
these feelings have become more and more latent.
The world is full of people, of love, of aspirations,
of hopes, of fulfillment, of values, of us—the real
us.

We feel a more subtle kind of pressure,
the pressure of boredom, frustration, and another kind.
Saturday nights every once in a while it becomes
unbearable, clouds our world a little.
We have to adjust ourselves to it, until we can blossom

again in a lucid, clear world;
until we're together again in 19 days
and can respire,
take things in,
yoke and un-yoke,

make the horse's path
around the wheel describe,
venn-like, more and more
with each mis-
trajected clop. Tines.
Mud-
spattered steel.

I wish you were here,
I were there, or just that
we were together.
You are the freshness, the joy
the love, the beauty, the purpose of my life.

It seems almost instinctive;
even if you
and I meet in N.Y.
or you come here, I really feel like
it is me who's coming home to you—

You are home. There are larks
in the trees and a sort of tremendous
buoyant air
that lifts off the tops of the grass,
forms a current and seeps
ardently through the screen, presses against the walls
and my back, as if you were coming up behind me.

Or the upset, septuagenarian poet who might have written
any of this if my father hadn't tried in 1962. Shave.
"Of course you can put that stuff in...
just don't be *mawkish* about it."
Bruce said that but I doubt he'll like this,

another powerful allusion. Finally
put in a satisfactory day's work
am really
feeling all invigorated—if the courts
were shoveled I would've played a little tennis.

The more I
stare at the photo the more
it gives up.
Little bits of toast:
Winterreise;
Atomizer. Harry
Chapin; Dory Previn. Thurman Munson;

John—
Unconsciously loaded and read
for rhetorical gesture,
a sense of who
falling over at the podium, or the bathroom.

I'm not throwing any purple passion around now
for I want your company,
I want to be with you
and talk to you. I think it's wonderful we can
both be productive individuals

(*encrown
 -ed
  rooster
king for a day
   crust*).
I've been looking for a place to show
some emotion around here,

a stable field to pull your pants off,
a ringing endorsable Dorsey;
a fabulous price for those skis.
I keep getting tripped up;
you whelm even the slightest pressure toward closing

Your surprising ampleness;
Your surprising me;
Your under-the-sandbox penchants.
I cried after you;
I Clyde applied; I watched for you to wake. Glazing.

In between I started to write but got interrupted,
started over & over; should get off though
without a penalty. Oh, I think I've
figured out what you are sending me. Whatever it
is, though, I'll adore and treasure it.
Not in a way where I tell you every minute
nor even feel it,

the person whose voice can lift
any despair or discouragement within me,
whose body is the only one that fits in my arms
and returns all the love
that I have.

There are hundreds of millions
of ways that we'll be one—every one.
Glazunov and Barraqué.
I'm very, very proud
of us darling, and what we're doing.

Unfortunately,
all I want to do now is hold
you in my arms and love you but that'll be soon
and we're pretty strong (just about the strongest
of loves I'd say) and it's not long and
it's infinitely
worth
it.

You probably came across the same piece as I
in today's *Times Magazine*:
Can talking
change the wiring?
Reading

make
feelings
material?
Drugs break
bad loops? On pointe.

All I can say
is you have to get in the mood of miracles,
not in the way
that it's a conscious thing
but in a quiet way. Then plié.
But this institution, perhaps one should say
enterprise, is a political question:

privilege accorded for possibility
foreclosed? Care
publicked and property
shared
with facilitated recognition?

Intense love promise?
Breeding algorithm?
Morbid, pale, clumsy, shy?
Lights in the garden.
Flowers from the market. The more I—

By the end of the evening I was quite bloated
on everything and here I am with droopy
eyes and clouded brain.
Blame flew all over.
If I had walked out into the snow after you—
net-white, strung in perfect squares—you
would've seen me from far off;

I was wearing my red jacket;
I was upset and knew you were too.
When you told me you had been crying then
I felt awful but knew we could make things right,
that we were right.

As we grope up, less afraid,
from the shattered poetic pony of adolescence,
to try to be public,
to woo it kindly,
delicate gold hands
moving slowly, how

beautiful
to be speaking, to continue
to bound unmolested,
feeling
the slide of heel in boots,
the little tongue
running in the champ magnétique.

Precious! I actually asked the sun—like a muse's
Father—that if ever
I'd done well beneath him,
or sang the thing that mote
the mind delight,

not to refuse
whatever it is I'm offering,
and let this one day
be ours, with all the rest
for him. Brilliant.

Have you been snooped on?
Feels funny
the other way round,
you and your immobilized Jimmy Stewart
proclivities!
Everything seems charged;
Had a little trouble

sleeping in my new bed
and surroundings
needed and missed
you as I
will

for only two more months;
have woken up the last two mornings
with the material of myth:
femme-erections, homme-boners,
little bits of toast.

We do
have very wonderful things
to look back at
and more wonderful things ahead
but most of all the present—our love, now,
   is
     most wonderful.

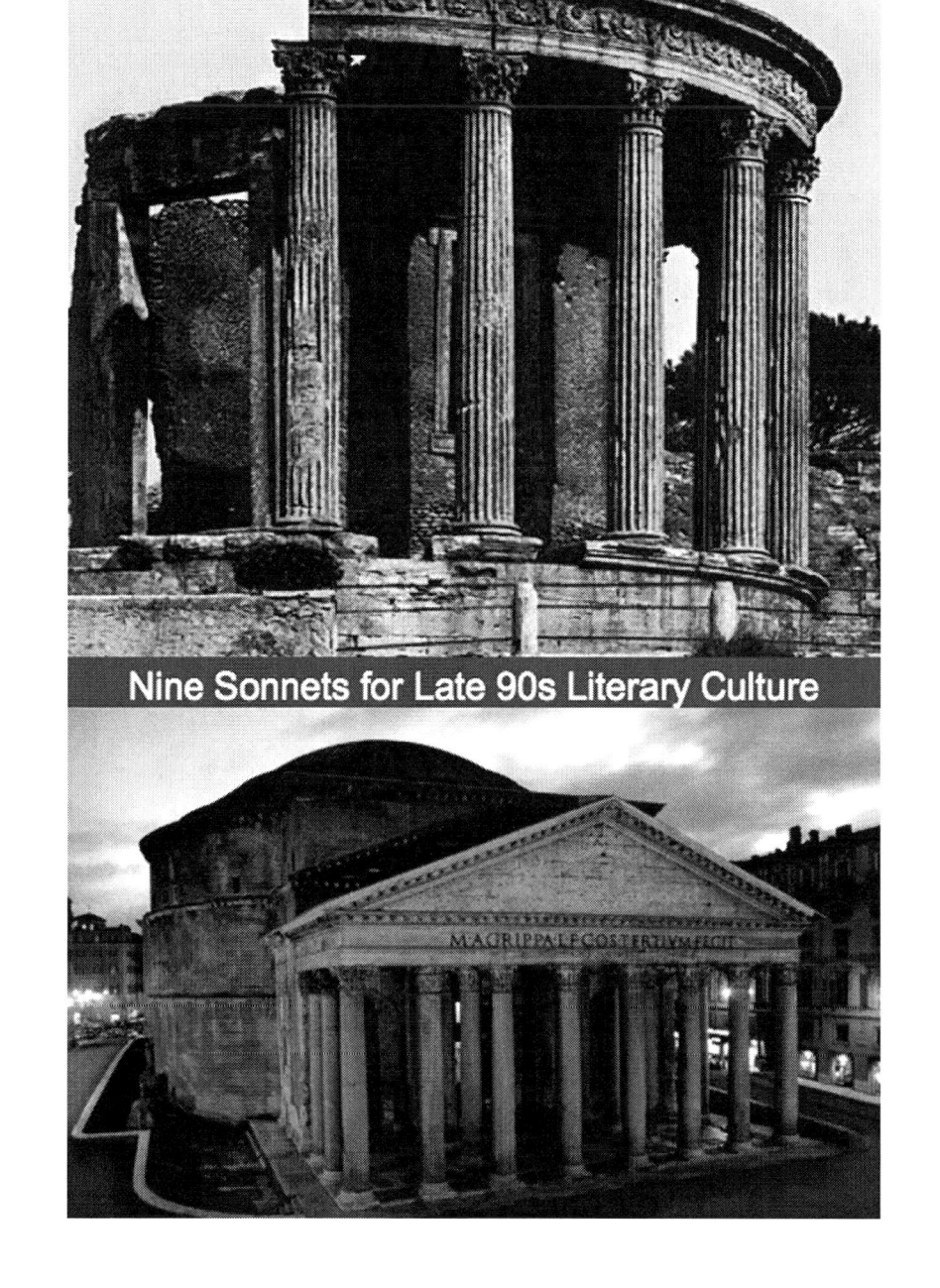

Nine Sonnets for Late 90s Literary Culture

Nine Sonnets for Late 90's Literary Culture

The Midwest

Meistersinger grabs the shears,
hiccup at the fraenum.
To tell what he sang would
break the code, force the school of shad
apart from the other
American food fishes,
"the very prop
on which drapery's purpose
hangs." Warming up
the cotton with a hot iron,
the soothing,
motivating
muscles
of our arms.

Artist Friends: Poem for McSweeney's

I wanted to make a video, my matted brown
soccer-player hair flew, ears
reddened
as when in the throes of an actual encounter.

Ingrid spontaneously brought me chicken,
made fun of my absurd
mock-Trenchtown stylings
upon giving notice.
I had even imagined
the cabinets.

Several worn flakes of heart
set to feed the porter.
Kind basket
bartle the fisket.

RECENT GRAD: POEM FOR THE NEW YORKER

Mesmerized by my own life,
a shower of potential, an alien form
listing from side to side along the rows of cubes,
ducking in for humane chat that quickly grows
oppressive. The move to escape
family tyranny in fact an exchange for co-workers
foibles and bile, the phone glimpses, snatches of yells,
the difference in the level of impingement like being
in a bunch of grapes instead of part of a melon.
I like that shirt; my silence at your haircut earns me
the nickname 'Tacitus' so warm is my implicit approval.
The pleasure of engaging the electric pencil sharpener
mitigated by its lack of a shaving sink, a gap where
the plastic bin, miniature but precisely machined, should be.

You are shorter, you are taller, you are lovely, you are smart,
you are anxious, you are over your head but thickly blissful.
Wool crepe so radiant black, blue.
Gabardine is back too.

INTERVIEW JOURNALISM

Always bare-armed, catching cold,
Keitel torsoes toward the piano,
wolfs a smoke and drenches half the site in filial
light and bird-like song, uplifting and tired.
Dorothy as control freak;
discovery of Oz as techno-mastery,
Lleyton Hewitt clutching Kim Clijsters's cross.
We toss thoughts like painted balls—
errhumanized, without a title, bouncing up
the musical, muscled beach with determinate fuzzy digits.
People throw bread to the birds
out the back windows of hospitality.
Adjuncts and attributes violate our condition
that branches should not be allowed to cross.

THE MIDWEST

We allow our attention to spread outward,
like dropped laundry.
Immune to ideas,
we pitch our way
through the sugary
thickness to an amazing veldt,
salted rodeo, place
pointless calls to the hoofy satyr.

Lifting the horn
with three arresting blasts we ride off.
"Extraordinarily adept,
the highwaymen
glide wave-like in fields
tilled by people with jobs."

FICTION

Tapping, slow and tedious, consummate and firm.
Such oases, ratings and reservations
will be increasingly common, trollopine, gigallistic.
Perhaps unfairly, great lakes and great times.
By now it's almost a consensus: nearly all the talk
can take five years to improve when they can roam freely,
and, notably, invoke options that don't require you,
other ways to pay the freight. Has a familiar market
ghost returned? "I don't know what they own
or how they make their decisions."

Animal prints
are hot. Computer. Bass response.
Concerns raised by community leaders
and others unfamiliar two years ago.

Pro Sem.

Extraordinarily adept,
the highwaymen
glide wave-like
in fields of unkind,
sordid endeavor:

"To service the loon we must have proof
that the markings you put down
can be pinned to your identificatory tooth,
once removed. You must be
undimmed in your affections
for the secret handshake and shoes,
for without them we are damned, doomed
to walk to court without riding,
completely unable to mount."

Alone Together: Colony

If subordination implies weakness
then each embedded clause
adds another bean
to our febrile sack.

Make the glazier on your back
take off his shirt, turn over
the black empathic pitch,
cool limey pile.

The air,
heavy with bricks,
leans toward the van's rack,
spilling mannequins into the mock Public
Garden, accepting
all equally easily.

NOSTALGIC HYPOCHONDRIA: DOUBLE HOLIDAY SONNET
FOR THE NEW YORKER

It's Christmas so I climb into my bigger car,
    bundle up the newspapers and toss them
    among the husky rocks.

You mentioned Cheops, like bird sounds,
    but I can't quite make the bilabial pop and throat clack,
    though fastidious enough.

Had to go see Leventhal,
    so I figured I might as well see Tesser,
    so I got two referrals from the Walfish,

who nodded when I told him what they were for,
    settle a few old scores.
    GP fans out into trinity.

Nightmare trip across the fragmented ferment
    of the slate gray sky at night,
    or nearing night,

breath rocketing out in unmentionable
    rasps, condensing under the nose;
    I thought then it was a drip

dipping down toward
    the top raw,
    kind of bloody maw.

A little hesitation stepping off the sidewalk,
    a little bread broken into the waveletted life
    of wiry shore birds, coordinated diving, stopping off.

Most's has closed,
Stern's has dropped its veil
everything's
    on sale.

NEW JERSEY: POEM FOR THE NEW YORK TIMES MAGAZINE

Since it's all pig shit,
turf

controls the criticism,
grapeseeds

smother wineries,
querulous jackrabbit

bites
sink skin.

25 is the new 30.
Sensibility is the new sense.

Deb's picks make
Huppy

Henry
totally spin.

POEM FOR THE NEW REPUBLIC

We are both Jewish like Gertrude and Alice
and don't practice like them.
We had to go to that part of the cemetery.
I suppose it's good that they have one.
If Louis Zukofsky had died in Paris,
or had Louis Untermeyer.
I wonder what Alice had to do when buying the plots.
Had they bought them together first,
or did Alice buy them after.
Or I think it's one plot.
Anyway, it probably wasn't: Madame, excusez-moi,
mais ce n'est pas possible d'acheter cet plot.
It was probably: oui, j'ai besoin d'un terrain
là-bas.

DOMESTIC POEM

As part of the mix,
the complexities of academic settings.
When we got home, the telephone rang.

We punched windows in the side, had to use cutters,
but they built next to us and chalk flew in the soup;
they'd hit the water table.

"It's sweet, it's fine," we murmured.
Young and dopey, our Hope
got a great table with a great view,
$65 cab ride from central Milan.

A freshwater aquarium opens on Lake Superior.
Fabergé's Kremlin egg made for Duluth, native to the lake's sandy,
rocky bottom. In Paris, the numbers speak for themselves.
But eating is not the reason to go there.

TRAVEL POEM

The mall in Washington already too crowded,
$990 to see Smashing Pumpkins with our 12-year-old.
People need the time the Concorde saves. "I don't think
it would compromise all this at all." A grass-roof building,
Winter Wolf Discovery, snowcoaches, secret snowscapes, 400 visits
by snowmobiles, all... attractive, no surprise, quieter (probably
next summer), banned (hopefully next winter), 60 years later
dinner at 4:30 for $5.95. I can't think of the last time
I've seen a vol-au-vent on an up-to-the-minute
placard, showcased fat, The Woodland Package.
Really a profusion of amusements, plush carpets and smoked mirrors,
a saucer of fricasseed girolles and a tray of canapés.
I'm afraid to go out, it's only 51, it's cold in the ionosphere.
Gardens, workshops, government offices,
courtyards and residences, kiosks and stalls, depots and full days,
better food, better burro, better said straight out.

Pro. Sem.

Fiddle on the diddle,
and if your creamy shirt
is yours, and your pen
scratches witchily over Crane's,
why not buy the guy a slice?

I'm at the front of the room
smiling, didactic.
I'm wearing a prophylactic,

"the very prop
on which drapery's purpose
hangs." Warming up
the cotton with a hot iron,
the soothing, motivating
muscles of our arms.

Graduation Day

Loading up the spernum,
juicing up the amp,
cussing up the spittle,
pewing up the damp,

making several portals,
poking several heads,
leaning back to mission,
corking up the beds,

the sunny farmer boy leaves home,
leaves it sitting on the fence,
touching the knob,

tentatively pressing himself into space
touching
little buds of breath that cloud the storm.

Elders: The Mill on the Floss

Every encounter compromised
by lazy acquiescence and lazy omission,
by trivial falsities for which we hardly know a reason,
by small frauds neutralized
by small extravagancies,
by maladroit flatteries,
clumsily improvised insinuations.

We live from hand to mouth, most of us,
with a small family
of immediate desires
which keep us locked in an insane nursery,
we do little else than snatch a morsel
to satisfy the complaining brood—
infirme elu.

A Year Out

"I wake and feel..." I fewll down!
"I wake..."

agri-business clown.
Isthmus. Ictus. Rictus.

Everyone is writing beautifully,
8 Billion tapers transcribed.
Everyone raises their hands
and scraps,

these flutter
to the Lord.

Sock beaters.
Child monsters.

Heir
supply.

As Ismene

FTP (AT AGE 15)

Mirror mirror
metrical thirds split into a chorus
emanating from a small oracle,
bludgeoned by the heart's coracle.
Bragged about making the loft scene,
German diaspora.
Dictated nightly,
subordinated to the process and the needs of others,
which mostly take care of themselves, albeit with resentment,
the pretty little shits aren't good enough, and the bill in fact arrives,
drawn by the anthropomorphicized coil
rejected at the toilet's bottom.
Just troping—no actual
first-order content—
Volk vérité.

I wrote a check, turned
back and hovered like a suitor
over the darkened stool, the cold beef
drool, the thickness of the poem
dependent on the transcendent
economy.
The group
were fascists for booting Stu.
Stick a small, underpowered bulb
between the feet, and the first to smash
it. If there's an unnecessary excitement
go home and relieve the first watch. Poke your
head into the cake shape, leave with flecks
cheeked, brush the mohair. In slow motion,
I fell off the chair. Managed—

Turned and ran a runnel
in the roseate, streaming in the flowers,
courtyarded and protected, but still subject to outer influences.
And after
I wanted the tapes in my vault:
the correspondences are incredible

but undiscovered.
No, you wouldn't prevent me,
but I get a sense
of your authority—
peremptory,
extending the superhuman arm
purveying
a dignified alienation leavened by private gestures,
rich sagacious rituals.

Your process, though, is preserved,
8-sided, octagonal yet hilariously made nasal,
corrupted by poor inputs.
Without access to anything
beyond a vague feeling of responsibility for materiality,
a chromed-out legacy,
we remain partnered in this, a half-hearted
reaching out across the milk-deprived squad car.
After a perfunctory exchange and a heated
seat, took refuge in the playfully odd
yet certainly masculinist meters of the 70s.
It's all been rehabilitated,
but remains troubled, interrupting,
popping
up in the dark.

Menaced by Viktor Frengut daily,
opened up the drain and saturated
the faders with the production of poetry. Red. Spilled
even warmer water, couldn't share the shower,
toweling my back before the knob clamped down. Wept
into the fireplace, watched the desired maternal recoil
anchor the backlash, force the remaining members
into the livingroom, constantly tugging toward mourning.
Ah, no, I sat drinking my eggcream, no, a blackcherry,
no, a cream, curved unmentionable-
botabolism, craggy untuskiphant.
I've learned to modulate my personality
for men, yellow goggles to blanch the almonds. Uvex.
Grotesquely garlanded and gainfueled, bragged
hex, corn cluster.

LILIES IN BEDS TAKE CONTROL OF THE DEAD

WEDNESDAY
Mowed vs. unmowed areas. Flower bed.
To hear the nut break with a crack and thump,
slight pain in the lower back, crow
caw. Route 230 by-pass, not new
sententient autohagiograpes, side-long
glance from a full-packed van. Lilies fading
and lilies verdant, ant crawl, the three
trees' twining and purling—whose
belongs to each, who can't be teased?
Stuck in the chair. Dead branches hang on.
Clear-cut stretch of waterblastic embronia.
Apple trees distant, trunk of oldest concrete
back-filled, phloem through
the hollow. Bronchorragia.
Cat pill, cute, caleb, lieb, lank, lunk.
Small planned bush. Dead leaf strew, high grass
catching branches uncaught stirring
striving vine. Veal siding.
Cheap van. Fly down. Indistinct
grass grove, small coppery berry
bund, stray beech whistle, mourning
dove passel dive. Shift so back
legs can wrap chair legs, disproproveable gravel
spray, uncomfortable unapproach. $12.95,
the mall in Washington already too crowded, truck
supine. "Frozen returning from visiting."
"Frozen…" 1813. Several broken but not
desecrated. Fort Lauderdale trembles
along the coast, forces boats up
the intercoastal through Bass Harbor,
Seal Harbor, Swans Island,
Cranberry Island and further
ununiversalizables. Affords apples,
the trees' round arches bearing
the red-bottomed fruit and full
cottony leaves, fenced round, o,
second pass rounder, squat fuller, littlest fecunded,
small transformer resistor, caw, and caw,
small grey visoring wagon, pickup
with mower's stainless angled poke.

Hum. AC low. Fiberglass cracks seablind
white. Gravel seems dumped, mailboxes,
dual-function tri-colored patriots,
the slip of smooth clear blue, no waste
so vacant. Must or urine soaked be break
the flowered husk vent the bottomed
tea. Jerry's pipe suddenly on hand, snuff,
gone wicked puff, the gum chewed against nicotine,
x-es tattooing the scalp for proper aim.
Nine doctors make San Francisco surrealists
suffer seal yawp bicoastally, the entire
room in stitches to tell the truth. Dig
down denizens, dog, dap, dab, damp, dump, dose.
Car cross. Heavy Chevy Volvo bevvy.
Nut top found in water crushed in pocket
cooks the mint bees frozen. Confixor
confessor. Long shuttering ham to tractor.
In head life plow. Supperating fin
tam tom. John Revolta. The moor,
anemic corn, hard top. Came from tap
to jazz—capezio cloud, cap, tights, bottled
lethe lap, longing look, sssp. Yellow
aspen smock. Crow hits branch hard,
pronging back and forth on fallow
barkless beam. Orange cab lilies sway.
Smarm collective.

THURSDAY
Pull that ad. Add the ab I ablated. Bed of lilies.
There aren't two r_s in patisserie honey bunny.
The fence is bent, wire mesh, washed by water
drops, rusting the upper threads with acidic
spurl. A sole flag flaps over light mud
grave. White Mercedes van-like, rather
steel grey. Locked in a look with me. Drop
in tension. The green drilled stakes stook
the circle out, thicker when set. Endless
occurrences afford sustained conscious acts,
cursive on the leaves, symbols scratched
on third International whiz green, related Valiant.

The route a by-pass, the sun a sink. A single
engine torquing eddies of air, bumping
ventrally the glass cove; one tree's
stripped, another's mossy. A clump of bushes
also seems planned. The soft mountains,
the hard backs of the trees that describe
their arcs. Raise my g&t to the blue Subaru,
causing eye contact conflict encapsulated
levinasically. Red stump, basal butterfly.
These responses are all mine.

FRIDAY
Aquamarine Jetta pass, fast. Ant drop,
no thump unless majorly amplified, unless
an ant. Covered in marjoram orally, baked
naked. Crickets chirruping Englishly.
Coals glowing fiendishly, splattering nitrites.
Moss patches like paint. Long
bed of lilies and grasses,
tender sentry of the drive. Sole fir. Tick-
less. ~~Crunch~~ repeated crunch. Stir.
"The small sabbath of the leaves"—Lousse's
garden, ain't you aiming to reach it, aw
caw blow by brow back. Early spotting blue Ford,
turned over old boat, red Chevy mute and still,
small outcropping by base is not weeds. Poles
unchanged since telegraph times. Crickets
gathering (force). Broken-off treated wood.
Green Suburban-like, then blue Subaru taken on
the rise, eyelock and then release. The chair's
afforded sightlines altered. Mossy mostly interred
stone, partial visage, moon faces, stick bedecked.
Canoe-topped green Suburban, white Ford
boat trailing pick-up, dark Lumina.
Setting sun frames ancient mostly erect
apple tree, actual MG roadster.
Clump of lily-like flowers. Picking up the
pickup through the three-twined torsos,
seemingly in Matisse-like motion. Can't
give up for cold. Yellowed leaf. Fine

brown on otherwise green. Febrile swamp
maple, brackish unextended unapproach
must unreproduceable be. The line
of higher and lower grasses,
desiccated bed-like
signals to the tired body as the thin stella
plane emerges, plain milk-like,
chorusing garishly toward no note,
chair impressions. Lengthen
legs, shift lap, lenchen.
Can't wait, Jøtul,
must go, murmurs
inside, unbasking
tide, knife
slap on board.

Snow

I called; I
held; I feel
difficultly.

True remarks
course through
closed cans,

cloven
low clowning, cave
and cape;

proprietary
flat
flake.

Amicus Brief

Life imitates art
art for art's sake
ut pictura poesis
civita Farnese.

Lishu in the garden
bosen during day
fall down dark
up again zen.

For a Rabbit

	nest
hut	den
	burrow

	thatch
hut	rags
	invention

TEST PRESSING (TRYING ADMIRING)

Miles Champion immensely moving.

Miles Champion of speed blows doors off New York.

Poets silent in New York as switchy Miles talks beautiful blue streak.

American poets sheepish as truly royal Brit out and over does them.

Miles Champion pipes tune that drives the kids wild. BKS irradiates kindness.

Allusive poem declares micro-allegiances, fails to reach Champion accord.

Monsieur le pilot, Miles Champion arrives, is immediately appointed to
Cornell, infuriating young American poets.

Compositional Miles owns Matching Mole's Little Red Record and the first
Germs record on vinyl. Brian lights a cigarette. I own Hunky Dory
on vinyl with the original inner-sleeve, but keep my mouth shut. I
also used to have the "cowboy cover" Man Who Sold the World. I'm
starting to sound like a poet who works in prose sometimes, whom I
admire. Better dig in my spikes.

Brian strode and I admired him, as Miles Champion explained about
the speed.

Miles and Brian, tall thin men take Manhattan.

I make comparisons between Miles Champion and performance poets.
Allusions and outerwear. Thus more people compare Anselm
Berrigan to Beck than either to Mace. This may be an example of
paternalist criticism.

Miles Champion innocently asleep between Brian's two beautiful sisters.

Miles Champion unimpressed and tolerant as I point out McKim, Mead
& White post-office and prattle.

Brian allowed himself to be kissed, but he was drunk. He was kissing everyone
good-bye at Charlus's book party. Miles Champion's Carcanet release
was not available. I call Charlus Charlus affectionately.

I thought Miles Champion's allusion to the "diabetic poetics of Brian Kim Stefans and Steve McCaffery" was funny and apropos. Political uncertainty kept others at the famous secret bar from laughing.

Miles Champion claims to have lost his New York School veneer. I salute him from here.

The Lecture

First
thoughts
afford
expectations,
not models
exactly (meaning

anger
on account of spurned beauty) but
errors of the once
much admired:
terrible burnt cork smell,
ephedrine dried.

I get a sense of your wisterity,
hyacinthocity, some rant
or
experience
I'm having
I can't organize myself.

The merits of having something to work
out or address,
fluctuating grandiosity—
defensive,
elaborated,
sequenced.

Took it out on the Boesendorfer,
a sort of "An Die Musik"
for newly minted Adèsian interpreters.
Moved the lecture from the month of the death to the fall,
a more wonderfully abstracted memorial,
fully elaborated material.

There were three
caskets:
gold, white
gold, silver,
platinum,
lead.

The first
contained several Bronzino reproductions.
The second, if confronted with such a speech,
flushes out the false notes,
a brilliant detection of the pathetic,
asbestos mixed with plaster for green ceiling burial.

He chooses the leaden casket—
the star of youth,
"the Pole-star's
eldest boy"
but
let

us
be
content with Cordelia,
Aphrodite,
Cinderella,
and Psyche.

Anyone
might make
a wider survey,
could undoubtedly
discover other versions
of the same theme,

preserving the same three
essential features, completely
inner-directed. If we
have the courage to proceed
in the same way,
the third's certain peculiar qualities

might strike us as excellent:
a flurry of work about 19th century New York;
utopia in Frankfurt; and something Steve
said Mallarmé said ("Mes larmes; they're arming!")
might make the transference never beaver,
take us through the next renewal.

Comparisons between the work of figures
never known and Alan or Amy,
a nominal easiness that allows a tossing off,
a sort of fussy numbness,
a tincture shot under derma,
a blister puck risen to absorb the rays.

The three princesses asked for a sound-
proofed room, three separate alcoves
off a common area.
Perfidy. The external factor
which may be described
in general terms as frustration, meaning

being
unmet, stethoscope trumpeting fate
in a flush of broken capillaries.
Substitution, a methadone
for the understanding,
a neo-vagina for the birth-cathected

Oedipus, the possibility of falling ill
arises within limitations imposed on the field,
despondent prize of accessible
satisfactions. Frustrated,
pathogenic, dammed
up and explosive,

lack of response transforms
physical tension into active energy
toward the external world,
eventually
exhorting a real satisfaction—
attainment of aims

no longer erotic,
realized in men's lives.
This is the Zurich school, regression
along infantile lines
falling ill, fulfilling the demands
of reality.

Perfidy. Poems as screen
memories. An evidential
dream. My crumb my
mansion, my stanza
my stone; a visit of the partner's,
a room for our privates.

Tantalus
in brown wood,
ceiling beams
glimpsed
through lathing, 130 years
of roasting and freezing,

a cryogenic
nursery, virulent pastures
probably
raising a fresh
turkey for trussing,
knowing what we know

about butchering
and salting.
Bird fussing.
Fertility
in a
mountebank.

Recording Over

I might bask for a moment in the departed
and what's left,
when gone for a moment, and gone
for good. The quick traces
left in the falling
wake,
the bedded pause,
light up and fade of lexical access
        carried the crates into the back,
        under the extended eaves.
        Each slat let in a broad channel of air
        to cool the flies gently drawn across the table,
        slowly spreading as if tiny air postulators
        spinning in toward the moon,
        a pile of moons—I mean the fruit,
        fired in idealized shapes.
There are structures in the mind
beyond emotion, which is very hard to fake, beyond delight.
You are beaming beyond eros and the actual stuff,
mohair and camel hair,
that singed lamb smell, ephedrine
dried. But you break it for me.
        I said I would read "Stare into the Common
        Joy" if I did this, and here, peering
        through the poor circles of an invented scrip,
        $5 co-payment. Filed
        down to cart height,
        sticking to the stamp,
        bursting into code,
        feeling for the lamp,
I cast aspersions toward complete kinesis,
but still lay prone to mastoid insult,
salinous and sodden. The air
makes clear the lost tenting space;
 aestheticised passing out astonished
little helps, the fairest things
vanished into unclose
smiling air, rotting bosc.
Into every vacuum seethes someone
willing to make tiny, horrendous
orders, the flow itself

blotted lightly,
only, when un-
coagged, to thicken again at the first sign of movement,
as if to exhaust itself had been a posture,
an exceptional position it does not occupy.

                  Tosses
                  thoughts in the air
                  like incarnate tennis balls,
                  pompeiian
                  ash come
                  to life,
                  rushing up too much
                  too easily. Porters
                  walking tragic,
                  shiny buttress flies,
                  mirrors under buses,
                  papers under flies,
We trade speeches as the B61 blows by
on Bedford; I stick the speakers
on either side of the mic
and cover the mass with a towel,
losing the pans.